Goosebumps

The Cuckoo Clock of Doom

Under the face of the clock I saw another door. A big door. I touched its gold knob.

What's behind this door? I wondered. Maybe the gears of the clock, or a pendulum.

I glanced over my shoulder again. No one was looking. No problem if I just peeked behind that big clock door.

I tugged on the gold knob. The door was stuck. I pulled harder.

The door flew open.

I let out a scream as an ugly green monster burst out of the clock. It grabbed me and knocked me to the floor.

Goosebumps

The Cuckoo Clock of Doom

R.L. Stine

Scholastic Children's Books,
Commonwealth House, 1-19 New Oxford Street, London WC1A 1NU
a division of Scholastic Ltd
London ~ New York ~ Toronto ~ Sydney ~ Auckland

First published in the USA by Scholastic Inc., 1995
First published in the UK by Scholastic Ltd, 1996

ISBN 0 590 13478 7

Typeset by Contour Typesetters, Southall, London
Printed by Cox & Wyman Ltd, Reading, Berks.

10 9 8 7 6 5 4 3 2

"Michael, your shoe's untied."

My sister, Tara, sat on the front steps, grinning at me. Another one of her dumb jokes.

I'm not an idiot. I knew better than to look down at my shoe. If I did, she'd slap me under the chin or something.

"I'm not falling for that old trick," I told her.

Mum had just called me and the brat inside for dinner. An hour before she had made us go outside because she couldn't stand our fighting any more.

It was impossible not to fight with Tara.

When it comes to stupid tricks, Tara never knows when to quit. "I'm not kidding," she insisted. "Your shoe's untied. You're going to trip."

"Knock it off, Tara," I said. I started up the front steps.

My left shoe seemed to cling to the cement. I pulled it up with a jerk.

1

"Yuck!" I'd stepped on something sticky.

I glanced at Tara. She's a skinny little squirt, with a wide red mouth like a clown's and stringy brown hair that she wears in two pigtails.

Everyone says she looks exactly like me. I hate it when they say that. My brown hair is not stringy, for one thing. It's short and thick. And my mouth is normal-sized. No one has ever said I look like a clown.

I'm a little short for my age, but not skinny.

I do *not* look like Tara.

She was watching me, giggling. "You'd better look down," she taunted in her singsong voice.

I glanced down at my shoe. It wasn't untied, of course. But I'd just stepped on a huge wad of gum. If I had looked down to check my shoe-laces, I would have seen it.

But Tara knew I *wouldn't* look down. Not if she told me to.

Tricked by Tara the Terror again.

"You're going to get it, Tara," I grumbled. I tried to grab her, but she dodged out of reach and ran into the house.

I chased her into the kitchen. She screamed and hid behind my mother.

"Mum! Hide me! Michael's going to get me!" she shrieked.

As if she were afraid of me. Fat chance.

"Michael Webster!" Mum scolded. "Stop chasing your little sister."

She glanced at my feet and added, "Is that gum on your shoe? Oh, Michael, you're tracking it all over the floor!"

"Tara *made* me step on it!" I whined.

Mum frowned. "Do you expect me to believe that? Michael, you're fibbing again."

"I am not!" I cried.

Mum shook her head in disgust. "If you're going to tell a lie, Michael, at least make it a good one."

Tara peeked out from behind Mum and taunted me. "Yeah, *Michael*."

Then she laughed. She loved this.

She's always getting me into trouble. My parents always blame me for stuff that's *her* fault. But does Tara ever do anything wrong? Oh, *no*, never. She's a perfect angel. Not a bad bone in her body.

I'm twelve. Tara's seven. She's made the last seven years of my life miserable.

Too bad I don't remember the first five very well. The pre-Tara years. They must have been awesome! Quiet and peaceful—and fun!

I went out to the back porch and scraped the sticky gum off my shoe. I heard the doorbell ring and Dad calling, "It's here! I'll get it."

Inside, everybody gathered around the front door. Two men were struggling to carry something heavy into the house. Something long and narrow and wrapped with padded grey cloth.

3

"Careful," Dad warned them. "It's very old. Bring it in here."

Dad let the delivery guys into the den. They set the thing down on one end and began to unwrap it. It was about as wide as me and maybe thirty centimetres taller.

"What is it?" Tara asked.

Dad didn't answer right away. He rubbed his hands together in anticipation. Our cat, Bubba, slinked into the room and rubbed against Dad's legs.

The grey cloth fell away, and I saw a very fancy old clock. It was mostly black but painted with lots of silver, gold and blue designs, and decorated with scrolls, carvings, knobs and buttons.

The clock itself had a white face with gold hands and gold Roman numerals. I saw little secret doors hidden under the paint designs, and a big door in the middle of the clock.

The delivery guys gathered up the grey padding. Dad gave them some money, and they left.

"Isn't it great?" Dad gushed. "It's an antique cuckoo clock. It was a bargain. You know that shop opposite my office, Anthony's Antiques and Stuff?"

We all nodded.

"It's been in the shop for fifteen years," Dad told us, patting the clock. "Every time I pass

Anthony's, I stop and stare at it. I've always loved it. Anthony finally put it on sale."

"Cool," Tara said.

"But you've been bargaining with Anthony for years, and he always refused to lower the price," Mum said. "Why now?"

Dad's face lit up. "Well, today I went into the shop at lunchtime, and Anthony told me he'd discovered a tiny flaw on the clock. Something wrong with it."

I scanned the clock. "Where?"

"He wouldn't say. Do you see anything, kids?"

Tara and I began to search the clock for flaws. All the numbers on the face were correct, and both the hands were in place. I didn't see any chips or scratches.

"I don't see anything wrong with it," Tara said.

"Me, neither," I added.

"Neither do I," Dad agreed. "I don't know what Anthony's talking about. I told him I wanted to buy the clock anyway. He tried to talk me out of it, but I insisted. If the flaw is so tiny we don't even notice it, what difference does it make? Anyway, I really do love this thing."

Mum cleared her throat. "I don't know, dear. Do you think it really belongs in the den?" I could tell by her face that she didn't like the clock as much as Dad did.

5

"Where else could we put it?" Dad asked.

"Well—maybe the garage?"

Dad laughed. "I get it—you're joking!"

Mum shook her head. She wasn't joking. But she didn't say anything more.

"I think this clock is just what the den needs, honey," Dad added.

On the right side of the clock I saw a little dial. It had a gold face and looked like a miniature clock. But it had only one hand.

Tiny numbers were painted in black along the outside of the dial, starting at 1800 and ending at 2000. The thin gold hand pointed to one of the numbers: 1995.

The hand didn't move. Beneath the dial, a little gold button had been set into the wood.

"Don't touch that button, Michael," Dad warned. "This dial tells the current year. The button moves the hand to change the year."

"That's kind of silly," Mum said. "Who ever forgets what year it is?"

Dad ignored her. "See, the clock was built in 1800, where the dial starts. Every year the pointer moves one notch to show the date."

"So why does it stop at two thousand?" Tara asked.

Dad shrugged. "I don't know. I guess the clockmaker couldn't imagine the year two thousand would ever come. Or maybe he figured the clock wouldn't last that long."

"Maybe he thought the world would blow up in 1999," I suggested.

"Could be," Dad said. "Anyway, please don't touch the dial. In fact, I don't want anyone touching the clock at all. It's very old and very, very delicate. Okay?"

"Okay, Dad," Tara said.

"I won't touch it," I promised.

"Look," Mum said, pointing at the clock. "It's six o'clock. Dinner's almost—"

Mum was interrupted by a loud gong. A little door just over the clock face slid open—and a bird flew out. It had the meanest bird face I ever saw—and it dived for my head.

I screamed. "It's alive!"

Cuckoo! Cuckoo!

The bird flapped its yellow feathers. Its eerie, bright blue eyes glared at me. It squawked six times. Then it jumped back inside the clock. The little door slid shut.

"It's not alive, Michael," Dad said, laughing. "It sure is real-looking, though, isn't it? Wow!"

"You birdbrain!" Tara teased. "You were scared! Scared of a cuckoo clock!" She reached out and pinched me.

"Get off me," I growled. I shoved her away.

"Michael, don't push your sister," Mum said. "You don't realize how strong you are. You could hurt her."

"Yeah, Michael," Tara said.

Dad kept admiring the clock. He could hardly take his eyes off it. "I'm not surprised the cuckoo startled you," he said. "There's something special about this clock. It comes from the

Black Forest of Germany. It's supposed to be enchanted."

"Enchanted?" I echoed. "You mean, magic? How?"

"Legend has it that the man who built this clock had magical powers. He put a spell on the clock. They say if you know the secret, you can use the clock to go back in time."

Mum scoffed. "Did Anthony tell you that? What a great way to sell an old clock. Claim it has magic powers!"

Dad wouldn't let her spoil his fun. "You never know," he said. "It could be true. Why not?"

"I think it's true," Tara said.

"Herman, I wish you wouldn't tell the kids these wild stories," Mum chided. "It's not good for them. And it only encourages Michael. He's always making things up, telling fibs and impossible stories. I think he gets it from you."

I protested. "I don't make things up! I *always* tell the truth!"

How could Mum say that about me?

"I don't think it hurts the kids to use their imaginations once in a while," Dad said.

"Imagination is one thing," Mum said. "Lies and fibs are something else."

I fumed. Mum was so unfair to me. The worst part was the expression of victory on Tara's face. Making me look bad was her mission in life. I wanted to wipe that smirk off her face for ever.

"Dinner's almost ready," Mum announced, leaving the den. The cat followed her. "Michael, Tara—go and wash your hands."

"And remember," Dad warned. "No one touches the clock."

"Okay, Dad," I said.

Dinner smelled good. I started for the bathroom to wash. As I passed Tara, she stomped hard on my foot.

"Ow!" I yelled.

"Michael!" Dad barked. "Stop making so much noise."

"But, Dad, Tara stomped on my foot."

"It couldn't have hurt that much, Michael. She's a lot smaller than you are."

My foot throbbed. I limped to the bathroom. Tara followed me.

"You're such a baby," she taunted.

"Be quiet, Tara," I said. How did I get the worst sister in the world?

We had pasta with broccoli and tomato sauce for dinner. Mum was on a big no-meat, low-fat kick. I didn't mind. Pasta was better than what we'd had the night before—lentil soup.

"You know, honey," Dad complained to Mum, "a hamburger now and then never hurt anybody."

"I disagree," Mum said. She didn't have to say more. We'd all heard her lectures about meat and fat and chemicals before.

Dad covered his pasta with a thick layer of Parmesan cheese.

"Maybe the den should be off limits for a while," Dad suggested. "I hate to think of you two playing in there and breaking the clock."

"But, Dad, I have to do my homework in the den tonight," I said. "I'm doing a report on 'Transportation in Many Lands'. And I need to use the encyclopaedia."

"Can't you take it up to your room?" Dad asked.

"The whole encyclopaedia?"

Dad sighed. "No, I guess you can't. Well, all right. You can use the den tonight."

"I need to use the encyclopaedia, too," Tara announced.

"You do not," I snapped. She wanted to hang around the den and bug me, that was all.

"I do, too. I'm supposed to read about the gold rush."

"You're making that up. You don't study the gold rush in the second grade. That's not until fourth."

"What do you know about it? Mrs Dolin is teaching us the gold rush *now*. Maybe I'm in a smarter class than you were."

11

Mum said, "Michael, really. If Tara says she needs to use the encyclopaedia, why start a fight about it?"

I sighed and stuffed a forkful of pasta in my mouth. Tara stuck her tongue out at me.

There's no point in talking, I thought. All it does is get me into trouble.

I lugged my backpack into the den after dinner. No sign of Tara—yet. Maybe I'd be able to get some homework done before she came in and started pestering me.

I dumped my books on Dad's desk. The clock caught my eye. It wasn't pretty—kind of ugly, really. But I liked looking at all those scrolls and buttons and knobs. It really did seem as if the clock could be magic.

I thought about the flaw Dad had mentioned. I wondered what it was. Some kind of bump? A missing notch on one of the gears? Maybe a piece of chipped paint?

I glanced back at the door to the den. Bubba wandered through it, purring. I petted him.

Mum and Dad were still in the kitchen, cleaning up after dinner. I didn't think it would matter if I just looked at the clock a little.

Careful not to touch any buttons, I stared at the dial that showed the year. I ran my fingers along a curve of silver at the edge of the clock. I glanced at the little door over the face of the clock. I knew the cuckoo sat behind the door, waiting to leap out at the right time.

I didn't want to be surprised by the bird again. I checked the time. Five minutes to eight.

Under the face of the clock I saw another door. A big door. I touched its gold knob.

What's behind this door? I wondered. Maybe the gears of the clock, or a pendulum.

I glanced over my shoulder again. No one was looking. No problem if I just peeked behind that big clock door.

I tugged on the gold knob. The door was stuck. I pulled harder.

The door flew open.

I let out a scream as an ugly green monster burst out of the clock. It grabbed me and knocked me to the floor.

"Mum! Dad! Help!" I shrieked.

The monster raised its long claws over me. I covered my face, waiting to be slashed.

"Goochy goochy goo!" The monster giggled and tickled me with its claws.

I opened my eyes. Tara! Tara in her old Halloween costume!

She rolled on the floor, giggling. "You're so easy to scare!" she shouted. "You should have seen your face when I jumped out of the clock!"

"It's not funny!" I cried. "It's—"

Gong.

Cuckoo, cuckoo, cuckoo, cuckoo!

The bird popped out of the clock and started cuckoo-ing. Okay, I admit it scared me again. But did Tara have to clutch her sides, laughing at me that way?

"What's going on in here?" Dad stood in the doorway, glaring down at us.

14

He pointed at the clock. "What's that door doing open? Michael, I *told* you to stay away from the clock!"

"ME?" I cried.

"He was trying to catch the cuckoo," Tara lied.

"I *thought* so," Dad said.

"Dad, that's not true! Tara's the one who—"

"Enough of that, Michael. I'm sick of hearing you blame Tara every time you do something wrong. Maybe your mother is right. Maybe I have been encouraging your imagination a little too much."

"That's not fair!" I yelled. "I don't have any imagination! I *never* make anything up!"

"Dad, he's lying," Tara said. "I came in here and saw him playing with the clock. I tried to stop him."

Dad nodded, swallowing every word his precious Tara said.

There was nothing I could do. I stormed off to my room and slammed the door.

Tara was the biggest pain in the world, and she never got blamed for anything. She even ruined my birthday.

I turned twelve three days ago. Usually, people like their birthday. It's supposed to be fun, right?

Not for me. Tara made sure my birthday was

15

the worst day of my life. Or at least *one* of the worst.

First, she ruined my present.

I could tell my parents were very excited about this present. My mother kept hopping around like a chicken, saying, "Don't go in the garage, Michael! Whatever you do, don't go in the garage!"

I knew she'd hidden my present in there. But just to torture her, I asked, "Why not? Why can't I go in the garage? The lock on my bedroom door is broken, and I need to borrow one of Dad's tools. . ."

"No, no!" Mum exclaimed. "Tell your father to fix the lock. He'll get the tools. You can't go in there, because . . . well . . . there's a huge mound of rubbish in there. It really stinks. It smells so bad, you could get sick from it!"

Sad, isn't it? And she thinks I get my "imagination" from Dad!

"All right, Mum," I promised. "I won't go in the garage."

And I didn't—even though the lock on my door really was broken. I didn't want to spoil whatever surprise they had cooked up.

They were throwing me a big birthday party that afternoon. A bunch of kids from school were coming over. Mum baked a cake and made snacks for the party. Dad ran around the house, setting up chairs and hanging crêpe paper.

"Dad, would you mind fixing the lock on my door?" I asked.

I like my privacy—and I *need* that lock. Tara had broken it a week earlier. She'd been trying to kickbox the door down.

"Sure, Michael," Dad agreed. "Anything you say. After all, you're the birthday boy."

"Thanks."

Dad took the toolbox upstairs and worked on the lock. Tara lounged around the dining room making trouble. As soon as Dad was gone, she pulled down a crêpe paper streamer and left it lying on the floor.

Dad fixed the lock and returned the tools to the garage. As he passed through the dining room, he noticed the torn-down streamer.

"Why won't this crêpe paper stay up?" he mumbled. He taped it back up. A few minutes later, Tara tore it down again.

"I know what you're doing, Tara," I told her. "Stop trying to wreck my birthday."

"I don't have to wreck it," she said. "It's bad all by itself—just because it's the day you were born." She pretended to shudder in horror.

I ignored her. It was my birthday. Nothing could keep me from having fun, not even Tara.

That's what I *thought*.

About half an hour before the party, Mum and Dad called me into the garage.

I pretended to go along with Mum's silly story. "What about the horrible rubbish?"

"Oh, that," Mum clucked. "I made it up."

"Really?" I said. "Wow. It was so believable."

"If you believed that, you must be a moron," Tara said.

Dad threw open the garage door. I stepped inside.

There stood a brand-new 21-speed bike. The bike I'd wanted for a long time.

The coolest bike I'd ever seen!

"Do you like it?" Mum asked.

"I love it!" I cried. "It's awesome! Thanks!"

"Cool bike, Mike," Tara said. "Mum, I want one of these for *my* birthday."

Before I could stop her, she climbed up on the seat of my new bike.

"Tara, get off!" I yelled.

She didn't listen. She tried to reach her feet to the pedals, but her legs were too short. The bike fell over.

"Tara!" Mum cried, running to the little brat's side. "Are you hurt?"

Tara stood up and brushed herself off. "I'm okay. I scraped my knee a little, though."

I picked up my bike and inspected it. It was no longer perfectly shiny and black. There was a huge white scratch across the middle bar.

It was practically ruined.

"Tara, you wrecked my bike!"

"Let's not get overexcited, Michael," Dad said. "It's only a scratch."

"Don't you even care about your sister?" Mum asked. "She could've been hurt!"

"It's her own fault! She shouldn't have touched my bike in the first place!"

"Michael, you have a lot to learn about being a good brother," Dad said.

They make me so mad sometimes!

"Let's go inside," Mum said. "Your friends will be here soon."

The party. I thought the party would make me feel better. After all, there would be cake, presents, and my best friends. What could go wrong?

It started out okay. One by one my friends arrived, and they all brought me presents. I'd invited five guys: David, Josh, Michael B., Henry and Lars; and three girls: Ceecee, Rosie and Mona.

I wasn't so crazy about Ceecee and Rosie, but I really liked Mona. She has long, shiny brown hair and a turned-up nose that's kind of cute. She's tall, and good at basketball. There's something sort of cool about her.

Ceecee and Rosie are Mona's best friends. I had to invite them if I was going to invite Mona. They always go everywhere together.

Ceecee, Rosie and Mona arrived all at once.

They took off their jackets. Mona was wearing pink dungarees over a white turtleneck. She looked great. I didn't care what the other girls were wearing.

"Happy birthday, Michael!" they all called out at the door.

"Thanks," I said.

They each handed me a gift. Mona's was small and flat and wrapped in silver paper. Probably a CD, I figured. But which one? What kind of CD would a girl like Mona think a guy like me would like?

I set the presents on top of the pile in the living room.

"Hey, Michael—what did your parents give you?" David asked.

"Just a bike," I said, trying to be cool about it. "A twenty-one speed."

I put on a CD. Mum and Tara brought in plates of sandwiches. Mum went back to the kitchen, but Tara stayed.

"Your little sister is so cute," Mona said.

"Not once you get to know her," I muttered.

"Michael! That's not very nice," Mona said.

"He's a terrible big brother," Tara told her. "He yells at me all the time."

"I do not! Get lost, Tara."

"I don't have to." She stuck her tongue out at me.

20

"Let her stay, Michael," Mona said. "She's not bothering anybody."

"Hey, Mona," Tara chirped. "You know, Michael really likes you."

Mona's eyes widened. "He does?"

My face got red-hot. I glared at Tara. I wanted to strangle her right then and there. But I couldn't—too many witnesses.

Mona started laughing. Ceecee and Rosie laughed, too. Luckily, the guys didn't hear this. They were around the CD player, skipping from cut to cut.

What could I say? I *did* like Mona. I couldn't deny it—it would hurt her feelings. But I couldn't admit it, either.

I wanted to die. I wanted to sink through the floor and die.

"Michael, your face is all red!" Mona cried.

Lars heard this and called out, "What did Webster do now?"

Some of the guys call me by my last name.

I grabbed Tara and dragged her into the kitchen, Mona's laughter ringing in my ears.

"Thanks a lot, Tara," I whispered. "Why did you have to tell Mona I like her?"

"It's true, isn't it?" the brat said. "I always tell the truth."

"Yeah, right!"

"Michael—" Mum interrupted. "Are you being mean to Tara again?"

I stormed out of the kitchen without answering her.

"Hey, Webster," Josh called when I returned to the living room. "Let's see your new bike."

Good, I thought. A way to get away from the girls.

I led them to the garage. They all stared at the bike and nodded at each other. They seemed really impressed. Then Henry grabbed the handlebars.

"Hey, what's this big scratch?" he said.

"I know," I explained. "My sister . . ."

I stopped and shook my head. What was the use?

"Let's go back and open my presents," I suggested.

We trooped back into the living room.

At least I've got more presents coming, I thought. Tara can't ruin those.

But Tara always find a way.

When I entered the living room, I found Tara sitting in the middle of a pile of torn-up wrapping paper. Rosie, Mona and Ceecee sat around her, watching.

Tara had opened all my presents for me.

Thanks so much, Tara.

She was ripping open the last present—Mona's.

"Look what Mona gave you, Michael!" Tara shouted.

It *was* a CD.

"I've heard there are some great *love* songs on it," Tara teased.

Everybody laughed. They all thought Tara was a riot.

Later, we all sat down in the dining room for cake and ice-cream. I carried the cake myself. Mum followed me, holding plates, candles, and matches.

It was my favourite kind of cake, chocolate-chocolate.

Balancing the cake in my hands, I stepped through the kitchen door and into the dining room.

I didn't see Tara pressed against the wall. I didn't see her stick her bratty little foot in the doorway.

I tripped. The cake flew out of my hands.

I landed on top of the cake. Face down. Of course.

Some kids gasped. Some tried to muffle their laughter.

I sat up and wiped the brown frosting from my eyes.

The first face I saw was Mona's. She was shaking with laughter.

Mum leaned over and scolded me. "What a mess! Michael, why don't you look where you're going?"

I listened to the laughter and stared at my ruined cake. I had no candles to blow out now. But it didn't matter. I decided to make a wish, anyway.

I wish I could start this birthday all over again.

I stood up, covered in gooey brown cake. My friends howled.

"You look like the Hulk!" Rosie cried.

Everybody laughed harder than ever.

They all had a great time at my party. Everyone did.

Except for me.

My birthday was bad—very bad. But ruining it wasn't the worst thing Tara did to me.

Nobody would believe the worst thing.

It happened the week before my birthday. Mona, Ceecee and Rosie were coming over. We all had parts in the school play, and planned to rehearse together at my house.

The play was a new version of *The Frog Prince*. Mona played the princess, and Ceecee and Rosie were her two silly sisters. Perfect casting, I thought.

I played the frog, before the princess kissed him and turns him into a prince. For some reason, our drama teacher didn't want me to play the prince. Josh got that part.

Anyway, I decided that the frog is a better part. Because Mona, the princess, kisses the *frog*, not the prince.

The girls would arrive any minute.

Tara sat on the rug in the den, torturing our cat, Bubba. Bubba hated Tara almost as much as I did.

Tara lifted Bubba by the hind legs, trying to

make him do a handstand. Bubba yowled and squirmed and wriggled away. But Tara caught him and made him do a handstand again.

"Stop that, Tara," I ordered.

"Why?" Tara said. "It's fun."

"You're hurting Bubba."

"No, I'm not. He likes it. See? He's smiling." She let go of his hind legs and grabbed him with one hand under his front legs. With the other hand she lifted the corners of his mouth and stretched them into a pained smile.

Bubba tried to bite her. He missed.

"Tara," I said, "let him go. And get out of here. My friends are coming over."

"No." Now Tara tried to make Bubba walk on his front paws. He fell and bumped his nose.

"Tara, stop it!" I cried. As I tried to take Bubba away from her, she let the cat go. Bubba meowed and scratched me across the arm.

"Ow!" I dropped Bubba. He ran away.

"Michael, what were you doing to that cat?" Mum stood in the doorway. Bubba slipped past her into the hall.

"Nothing! He scratched me!"

"Stop teasing him, and he won't scratch you," Mum scolded. She left, calling over her shoulder, "I'm going upstairs to lie down for a while. I have a headache."

The doorbell rang. "We'll get it, Mum!" I called.

I knew it must be the girls at the door. I wanted to surprise them in my frog costume, but I wasn't ready yet.

"Answer the door, Tara," I told the brat. "Tell Mona and the others to wait for me in the den. I'll be right back."

"Okay," Tara said. She trotted off to the front door. I hurried upstairs to change into my costume.

I pulled the costume out of my closet. I took off my trousers and shirt. I picked up the frog suit, trying to open the zipper. It was stuck.

I stood there in my underwear, tugging at the zipper. Then my bedroom door clicked open.

"Here he is, girls," I heard Tara say. "He told me to bring you upstairs."

No! I thought. *Please* don't let it be true!

I was afraid to look up. I knew what I'd see.

The door wide open. Mona, Ceecee, Rosie and Tara, staring at me in my underwear!

I forced myself to look. It was worse than I'd thought.

There they all stood—staring and laughing!

Tara laughed hardest of all. She laughed like a rotten little hyena.

You think that's bad? Wait. There's more.

Two days before the underwear disaster, I was

hanging around after school, playing basketball in the gym with Josh, Henry, and some other guys, including Kevin Flowers.

Kevin is a good player, big and tough. He is twice as tall as me! He loves basketball. The Duke Blue Devils are his favourite college team. He wears a Blue Devils cap to school every day.

While we were shooting baskets, I spied Tara hanging around the sidelines, where we'd all tossed our jackets and backpacks against the wall.

I got a bad feeling. I always do when Tara's around.

What's she doing there? I wondered.

Maybe her teacher kept her after school, and she's waiting for me to walk her home.

She's just trying to distract me, I told myself. Don't let her. Don't think about her. Just concentrate on the game.

I felt good. I actually sank a few baskets before the game ended. My side won. We had Kevin Flowers on our team, that's why.

We all jogged to the wall to get our packs. Tara was gone.

Funny, I thought. I guess she went home without me.

I hoisted my pack over my shoulder and said, "See you tomorrow, guys."

But Kevin's voice boomed through the gym. "Nobody move!"

We all froze.

"Where's my cap?" he demanded. "My Blue Devils cap is missing!"

I shrugged. *I* didn't know where his stupid cap was.

"Somebody took my cap," Kevin insisted. "Nobody leaves until we find it."

He grabbed Henry's backpack and started pawing through it. Everyone knows how much Henry loves that cap.

But Josh pointed at me. "Hey—what's that hanging out of Webster's pack?" he asked.

"My pack?" I cried. I glanced over my shoulder.

I saw a patch of blue sticking out of the zippered pocket.

My stomach lurched.

Kevin strode over to me and ripped the cap out of my pack.

"I don't know how it got there, Kevin," I insisted. "I swear—"

Kevin didn't wait to hear my excuses. He never was much of a listener.

I'll spare you the blood and gore. Let's just say my clothes didn't fit too well when Kevin got through taking me apart!

Josh and Henry helped me home. My mum didn't recognize me. My eyes and nose had traded places with my chin.

While I was in the bathroom cleaning myself

up, I caught a glimpse of Tara in the mirror. The bratty grin on her face told me all I needed to know.

"*You!*" I cried. "You put Kevin's cap in my pack! Didn't you!"

Tara just grinned. Yeah. She did it, all right.

"Why?" I demanded. "Why did you do it, Tara?"

Tara shrugged and tried to look innocent. "Was that Kevin's cap?" she said. "I thought it was yours."

"What a lie!" I cried. "I never wear a Duke cap, and you know it! You did that on purpose!"

I was so furious, I couldn't stand to look at her. I slammed the bathroom door in her face.

And of course I got in trouble for slamming the door.

Now you understand what I had to live with.

Now you know why I did the terrible thing that I did.

Anyone in my place would have done the same.

I stayed in my room that night, thinking hard. Plotting a way to get Tara in trouble.

But nothing came to me. At least, nothing good enough.

Then the clock arrived. A few days later, Tara did something that gave me an idea.

Tara couldn't stay away from the cuckoo clock. One afternoon, Dad caught Tara playing with the clock hands. She didn't get into any *real* trouble, of course—not sweet little Tara. But Dad did say, "I've got my eye on you, young lady. No more playing with the clock."

At last! I thought. At last Dad realizes that Tara's not a perfect angel. And at last I've found a way to get her into big trouble.

If something went wrong with the clock, I knew Tara would be blamed for it.

So I decided to make sure something *did* go wrong.

Tara deserved to get into trouble for the

hundreds of terrible things she did to me.

So *what* if just once she gets blamed for something she didn't do? I thought. It's only evening the score a little.

That night, after everybody was asleep, I sneaked downstairs to the den.

It was almost midnight. I crept up to the clock and waited.

One minute to go.

Thirty seconds.

Ten seconds.

Six, five, four, three, two, one . . .

The gong sounded.

Cuckoo! Cuckoo!

The yellow bird popped out. I grabbed it mid-cuckoo. It made short, strangling noises.

I twisted its head around, so it faced backwards. It looked really funny that way.

It finished out its twelve cuckoos, facing the wrong way.

I laughed to myself. When Dad saw it, he'd go *ballistic*!

The cuckoo slid back into its little window, still facing backwards.

This is going to drive Dad insane! I thought wickedly.

He'll be furious at Tara. He'll explode like a volcano!

Finally, Tara will know what it feels like to be blamed for something you didn't do.

I crept back upstairs. Not a sound. No one saw me.

I fell asleep that night a happy guy. There's nothing like revenge.

I slept late the next morning. I couldn't wait to see Dad blow up at Tara. I just hoped I hadn't missed it already.

I hurried downstairs. I checked the den.

The door stood open.

No one there. No sign of trouble yet.

Good, I thought. I haven't missed it.

I made my way into the kitchen, hungry. Mum, Dad and Tara sat around the table, piled with empty breakfast dishes.

As soon as they saw me, their faces lit up.

"Happy birthday!" they cried all at once.

"Very funny," I snapped. I opened a cabinet. "Is there any more cereal left?"

"Cereal!" Mum said. "Don't you want something special, like pancakes?"

I scratched my head. "Well, sure. Pancakes would be great."

This was a little strange. Usually if I woke up late, Mum said I had to get my own breakfast. And why should I want something special, anyway?

Mum mixed a fresh batch of pancake batter. "Don't go in the garage, Michael! Whatever you do, don't go in the garage!" She hopped up and down, all excited. Just as if it were my birthday again.

Weird.

"... there's a huge mound of rubbish in there," Mum was saying. "It really stinks. It smells so bad, you could get sick from it!"

"Mum, what's with the rubbish story?" I asked. "I didn't believe it the first time."

"Just don't go into the garage," she repeated.

Why was she saying this to me? Why was she acting so weird?

Dad excused himself, saying, "I've got a few important chores to do," in a strange, jolly way.

I shrugged and tried to eat my breakfast in peace. But after breakfast I passed through the dining room. Somebody had decorated it with crêpe paper. One strand had been torn down.

Weird. Totally weird.

Dad came into the room, toolbox in hand. He picked up the torn piece of crêpe paper and started to tape it back up again.

"Why won't this crêpe paper stay up?" he asked.

"Dad," I said. "Why are you covering the dining room with crêpe paper?"

Dad smiled. "Because it's your birthday, of course! Every birthday party needs crêpe paper.

Now, I bet you can't wait to see your present,
right?"

I stared at him.

What's going on here? I wondered.

Mum and Dad led me to the garage. Tara followed. They all acted as if they were really going to give me a birthday present.

Dad opened the garage door.

There it was. The bike.

It was perfectly shiny and new-looking. No scratches anywhere.

That must be a surprise, I thought. They figured out a way to get rid of the scratch somehow. Or maybe they got me another new bike!

"Do you like it?" Mum asked.

"It's awesome!" I replied.

Tara said, "Cool bike, Mike. Mum, I want one of these for *my* birthday."

Then she jumped up on the seat. The bike fell over on her. When we pulled it up, it had a big scratch on it.

Mum cried, "Tara! Are you hurt?"

I couldn't believe it. What a nightmare!

It was happening all over again. Exactly as it had happened on my birthday.

What's going on?

"What's wrong, Michael?" Dad asked. "Don't you like the bike?"

What could I say? I felt sick. I felt so confused.

Then it dawned on me.

It must have been my wish, I thought.

My birthday wish.

After Tara tripped me and I fell on my cake, I wished I could go back in time and start my birthday all over again.

Somehow my wish came true.

Wow! I thought. This is kind of cool.

"Let's go inside," Mum said. "The party guests will be here soon."

The party?

Oh, no.

Please no!

Do I have to live through that horrible party again?

Yes.

Yes, I had to live through the whole horrible nightmare again.

My friends all showed up, just like the first time.

I heard Tara say the awful words, "Hey, Mona. You know, Michael really likes you."

Mona said, "He does?"

You already knew that, Mona, I thought. Tara told you four days ago.

You were standing in that very same spot. Wearing those same pink dungarees.

Mona, Ceecee and Rosie cracked up.

I panicked. This can't go on, I thought.

My mother came in, carrying a tray of soda. I grabbed her.

"Mum," I begged. "Please take Tara away. Shut her up in her room or something!"

"Michael, why? Your sister wants to have fun, too."

"Mum—*please!*"

"Oh, Michael, you're being silly. Be nice to Tara. She won't bother you. She's just a little girl."

Mum left the room, stranding me with Tara and my friends.

She couldn't save me.

No one could.

I showed the guys my new bike. Henry said, "Hey, what's this big scratch?"

When we got back to the living room, there were all my presents, opened by Tara.

"Look what Mona gave you, Michael!" Tara shouted.

I know, I know, I thought. A CD. With great love songs on it.

"I've heard there are some great *love* songs on it," Tara repeated.

Everybody laughed.

It was just as bad as before.

No. Worse. Because I could see it all coming. And I couldn't stop it.

Could I?

"Michael," Mum called. "Come into the kitchen, please. It's time for the birthday cake!"

Here's the test, I thought, dragging myself into the kitchen.

I'll carry in the cake—but this time I won't trip.

I know Tara is going to try and trip me. I won't let her.

I won't make a fool of myself this time.

I don't have to. I don't have to repeat everything the same way.

Do I?

I stood in the kitchen, staring at the cake. I could hear my friends laughing and talking in the dining room. Tara was in there, too.

I knew she was standing just beyond the dining room door, waiting. Waiting to stick out her foot and trip me. Waiting to make me fall on my face and embarrass myself all over again.

Not this time.

I carefully picked up the cake in both hands. I started towards the dining room.

Mum followed, just as before.

I stopped in front of the entrance to the dining room. I glanced down.

No sign of Tara's foot.

Carefully, watching closely, I stepped through the door. One step.

So far, so good.

Another step. I stood inside the dining room now.

41

I'd made it! All I had to do was get to the table, about five steps away, and I'd be safe.

I took another step forward. Another.

Then I felt a tug on my foot.

Tara reached out from under the table.

So that was where she'd been hiding. I knew it now. But it was too late.

Everything seemed to move in slow motion. Like in a dream.

I heard an evil giggle.

She grabbed my foot.

Oh, no, I thought. It's happened.

I lost my balance.

As I fell, I turned my head and glanced back.

Tara sat under that table, smirking at me.

I wanted to kill her.

But first I had to fall on my face on a cake.

The cake flew out of my arms. I turned my head again.

Splat!

Everybody gasped with laughter. I sat up and wiped the frosting from my eyes.

Mona leaned over the table, laughing harder than anybody.

The second time was more embarrassing than the first.

I sat on the floor, my face covered with cake, thinking, how could I have been so stupid?

Why did I have to make that wish?

I'll never wish for anything ever again.

I cleaned myself up and managed to survive the rest of the party. When I went to bed that night, I thought, at least it's over.

I switched off the light and pulled the covers up high.

It's over, I repeated. I'll go to sleep, and everything will be back to normal in the morning.

I shut my eyes and fell asleep. But in my dreams, all night long, I saw scenes from my horrible birthday party. The nightmare party became a real nightmare.

There was Tara, telling Mona that I liked her. Mona's face loomed up large in my dreams, laughing, laughing. Ceecee and Rosie and the guys, all laughing right in my face.

I tripped and fell on top of the cake, over and over again.

I tossed and turned. Each dream was scarier than the last. Soon my friends looked like horrible monsters. And Tara was the most horrible of all. Her features melted into a blur as she laughed and laughed at me.

Wake up, I told myself. Wake up!

I dragged myself out of the nightmare world. I sat up in bed, in a cold sweat.

The room was still dark. I glanced at the clock.

Three o'clock in the morning.

I can't sleep, I thought miserably. I can't calm down.

I've got to tell Mum and Dad what happened. Maybe they can help.

Maybe they can make me feel better.

I climbed out of bed and hurried down the dark hall to their room. Their door was open a crack.

I pushed it open.

"Mum? Dad? Are you awake?"

Dad rolled over and grunted, "Huh?"

I shook Mum's shoulder. "Mum?"

Mum stirred. "What is it, Michael?" she whispered. She sat up and grabbed the clock radio. In the clock's dim blue glow I saw her squint, trying to read the time.

"It's three o'clock!" she cried.

Dad snorted and sat up suddenly. "Huh? What?"

"Mum, you've got to listen to me!" I whispered. "Something creepy happened today. Didn't you notice it?"

"Michael, what is this—"

"My birthday," I explained. "Tara ruined my birthday, and I wished I could have it all over again. I wanted to make it better. But I never thought the wish would come true! Then, today, it was my birthday again! And everything happened exactly the same. It was horrible!"

44

Dad rubbed his eyes. "That you, Michael?"

Mum patted him. "Go back to sleep, dear, Michael's just had a bad dream."

"No, Mum," I cried. "It wasn't a dream. It was real! My birthday happened twice! You were there, both times. Don't you understand?"

"Listen, Michael," Mum began. I heard impatience in her voice. "I know you're excited about your birthday, but it's two days away. Only two days to go—then it will be your birthday at last! Okay? So go back to bed now and get some sleep."

She kissed me good night. "Only two days till your birthday. Sweet dreams."

I staggered back to bed, my head spinning.

Two days until my birthday?

Hadn't I just lived through my birthday—twice?

I switched on the reading lamp and stared at the date on my watch. February third, it said.

My birthday is February fifth. My birthday was two days away.

Could it be true? Was time going backwards?

No, I thought. I must be going nuts.

I shook my head hard. I slapped myself a few times. Going back in time. I laughed at the idea.

It's impossible, I thought. Get a hold of yourself, Michael.

All I did was wish to celebrate my birthday over again—*once*.

I didn't wish to repeat my twelfth birthday

for the rest of my life!

But if that's what's happening, why is it now *two* days before my birthday? Why isn't it just the night before?

Maybe time really *is* going backwards, I thought. Maybe this has nothing to do with my wish.

But, then—why is this happening to me?

I racked my brains.

The clock. Dad's cuckoo clock.

I twisted the cuckoo's head backwards . . . went to bed . . . and when I woke up, time had gone backwards.

Could that be it? Did *I* do this?

Is Dad's clock really magic?

Maybe I shouldn't have turned that stupid bird backwards, I decided. It figures—I try to get Tara in trouble, and end up getting *myself* into a horrible mess.

Well, if that *is* what happened, it's easy enough to fix.

I'll just go downstairs and turn the cuckoo's head back around.

I tiptoed out of my room and down the stairs. My parents had probably fallen back to sleep already, but I didn't want to take any chances.

I definitely didn't want Dad to catch me fooling around with his precious clock.

My feet hit the cold, bare floor of the hall.

I crept into the den. I switched on a lamp.
I glanced around the room.
The cuckoo clock was gone!

"No!" I cried.

Had the clock been stolen?

Without the clock, how could I fix everything? How could I turn the bird's head around and make my life go forward again?

I raced upstairs. I didn't care who I woke up now.

"Mum! Dad!" I yelled. I burst into their room and shook Mum awake again.

"Michael, what is it?" She sounded furious. "It's the middle of the night. We're trying to get some sleep!"

Let them be angry, I thought. This was way more important.

"The cuckoo clock! It's gone!"

Dad rolled over. "What? Huh?"

"Michael, you've had another nightmare," Mum assured me.

"It's not a nightmare, Mum—it's true! Go downstairs and see for yourself! There's no cuckoo clock in the den!"

"Michael—listen to me. It was a dream."
Mum's voice was firm. "We don't own a cuckoo
clock. We never did."

I staggered backwards.

"It's just a dream. A bad dream," she said.

"But Dad bought it . . ."

I stopped.

I understood now.

The date was February third. Two days before
my birthday.

And *five* days before Dad bought the cuckoo
clock.

We were travelling back in time. Dad hadn't
bought the clock yet.

I felt sick.

Mum said, "Michael, are you all right?" She
climbed out of bed and pressed the back of her
hand against my forehead.

"You feel a little warm," she said, nicer
now that she thought I might be sick. "Come
on, let's get you to bed. I'll bet you have a fever—
and that's why you're having all these night-
mares."

Dad grunted again. "What? Sick?"

"I'll take care of it, Herman," Mum whispered.
"Go back to sleep."

She guided me back to bed. She thought I was
sick.

But I knew the truth.

I had made time move backwards. And the clock was gone.

How would I fix things now?

By the time I got to the kitchen the next morning, Mum, Dad and Tara had already eaten.

"Hurry up, Michael," Dad said. "You'll be late."

Being late for school didn't seem to matter much at the moment.

"Dad, please sit down for a second," I pleaded. "Just for a minute. It's important."

Dad sat, impatiently, on the edge of a kitchen chair. "Michael, what is it?"

"Mum, are you listening?" I asked.

"Sure, honey," Mum said. She put the milk in the refrigerator and busily wiped off the counter.

"This is going to sound weird," I began. "But I'm not kidding."

I paused. Dad waited. I could tell by the tension in his face he expected me to say something totally dopey.

I didn't disappoint him.

"Dad, time is going backwards. Every day I wake up—and it's an earlier day than the last!"

Dad's face drooped. "Michael, you have a wonderful imagination, but I'm really running

51

late. Can we talk about it when I get home from work tonight? Or why don't you write it down? You know I love reading science fiction stories."

"But, Dad—"

Mum said, "Did somebody remember to feed the cat?"

"*I* did it," Tara said. "Even though it's *supposed* to be *Michael's* job."

"Thanks, Tara," Mum said. "Let's hit the road, everybody."

I grabbed a muffin as Mum hustled us out the door.

They're too busy to understand right now, I reasoned as I hurried to school. Tonight, at dinner, when I have more time to explain . . .

I had lots of time to think about my problem during school. I'd lived through this day before, too. I'd already done all the work, heard all the lessons, eaten the lousy lunch.

When my maths teacher, Mr Parker, turned his back to the class, I knew what would happen next. I predicted it to the second. Kevin Flowers threw an eraser at him and hit him smack on the back of his black trousers.

Now Mr Parker is going to turn around . . . I thought, watching Mr Parker.

He turned around.

. . . now he'll yell at Kevin . . .

Mr Parker shouted, "Kevin Flowers—to the principal's office, now!"

. . . now Kevin will start yelling his head off.

"How do you know it was me!" Kevin yelled. "You didn't see me do anything!"

The rest of the scene happened as I remembered it. Mr Parker cowered a bit—Kevin is pretty big—but told Kevin to go to the principal's office again. Kevin kicked over an empty chair and threw his books across the room.

It was all so boring.

After school, I found Tara in the den, teasing Bubba. She lifted his hind legs and made him walk on his front paws.

"Tara, stop it!" I cried. I tried to take Bubba away from her. She let the cat go. Bubba meowed and scratched me across the arm.

"Ow!" I dropped Bubba. He ran away.

It felt very familiar. And painful.

"Michael, what were you doing to that cat?" Mum demanded.

"Nothing! He scratched me!"

"Stop teasing him, and he won't scratch you," Mum scolded.

The doorbell rang.

Oh, no.

Mona, Ceecee and Rosie. *The Frog Prince*.

The underwear.

I can't let it happen.

But my feet started taking me upstairs. I was walking like a robot to my room.

Why am I doing this? I asked myself.

I'll get my frog costume. The zipper will be stuck.

Tara will open the door, and I'll be standing there in my underpants.

Mona will laugh her head off. I'll want to sink through the floor.

I know all this will happen.

So why am I doing it?

Can't I stop myself?

Don't go upstairs, I begged myself. Don't go to your room.

You don't *have* to do this.

There must be a way to stop it, to control it.

I forced myself to turn around. I walked back down the steps. I sat down on the third step.

Tara answered the door, and soon the girls stood before me in the hall.

Okay, I thought. I'm controlling it. Already things are happening differently from before.

"Michael, where's your costume?" Mona asked. "I really want to see what your costume looks like."

"Uh, no you don't," I said, shrinking a little. "It's really ugly, and I don't want to scare you girls—"

"Don't be a jerk, Michael," Ceecee said. "Why would we be scared by a stupid frog costume?"

"And, anyway, I want to rehearse with it," Mona added. "I don't want to see the costume for the first time on-stage. I'll need to be prepared for it. I need to practise with the costume—and you in it."

"Come on, Michael," Tara put in. "Show them the costume. I want to see it, too."

I flashed her a dirty look. I knew what she had in mind.

"No," I insisted. "I can't do that."

"Why not?" Mona demanded.

"I just can't."

"He's shy!" Rosie exclaimed.

"He's embarrassed," Tara added.

"No, it's not that," I said. "It's just that . . . it's awfully hot in that costume, and—"

Mona leaned close to me. I smelled something sweet, like strawberries. It must've been the shampoo she used. "Come on, Michael," she said. "For me?"

"No."

She stamped her foot. "I won't rehearse our scenes unless you put on that costume!"

I sighed. I didn't see any way out of it. Mona wouldn't leave me alone until I put on that frog costume.

I gave in. "Okay."

"Hurray!" Tara cried. I gave her another dirty look.

All right, I thought. I may have put on the

costume. But that doesn't mean the girls have to see me in my underwear.

I can still keep that from happening.

I trudged up to my room. But this time, I locked the door.

Now try to embarrass me, Tara, I thought. You can't outsmart Michael Webster. No way.

The door was locked. I felt sure I was safe.

I took off my jeans and my shirt. I dragged the frog costume out of the closet.

I tugged on the zipper. It was stuck.

Just like the last time.

But this time it's okay, I told myself. The door is locked. I have privacy.

Then the door flew open.

I stood helplessly in my underwear. Mona, Rosie and Ceecee stared at me. Then they screamed and started laughing.

"Tara!" I yelled. "The door was locked!"

"No, it wasn't," Tara replied. "The lock's broken, remember?"

"No!" I cried. "Dad fixed it . . . he fixed it . . ."

I tried to remember when Dad had fixed the lock on my bedroom door.

Oh, right.

It was after the underwear nightmare. On my birthday.

So it hadn't happened yet.

How was I supposed to keep all this straight?

Oh, no, I thought. I'm doomed.

Time is all messed up. And I have no way of stopping it.

I began to shake. This was too frightening.

Where would it end? I had no idea. It was getting scarier by the minute.

I could hardly eat dinner that night. I'd eaten it before, of course, and hadn't liked it the first time. Peas, carrots and mushrooms. With brown rice.

I picked at the rice and the carrots. I never eat peas. I slipped them into my napkin when Mum and Dad weren't looking.

I watched Mum, Dad and Tara eat dinner as if nothing were wrong. They sat calmly around the table, saying the same things they'd said last time.

Mum and Dad must notice that something is weird, I thought. They must.

So why don't they say anything about it?

I waited for Dad to finish telling us about his day at work. Then I brought up the subject again. I decided to take it slowly.

"Mum? Dad? Doesn't this dinner seem a little bit familiar?"

"I'll say," Dad replied. "It reminds me of the lunch we ate at that vegetarian restaurant last month. Ugh."

58

Mum glared at him, then at me. "What are you trying to tell us, Michael?" she said frostily. "Are you tired of eating healthy food?"

"I am," Dad said.

"Me, too," Tara chimed in.

"No. No way," I insisted. "You don't understand. I don't mean that we've eaten food like this before. I mean that we have eaten *this very meal* before. We're eating it twice."

Dad frowned. "No weird theories at the dinner table, please, Michael."

They weren't getting it. I ploughed ahead. "It's not just this dinner. It's this whole day. Haven't you noticed? We're doing everything over! Time is going backwards!"

"Shut up, Michael," Tara said. "This is so boring. Can't we talk about something else?"

"Tara," Mom scolded, "don't say 'shut up'." She turned to me. "Have you been reading those comic books again?"

I grew very frustrated. "You're not listening to me!" I cried. "Tomorrow is going to be yesterday, and the day after that will be the day before! Everything is going backwards!"

Mum and Dad exchanged glances. They seemed to be sharing a secret.

They *do* know something, I thought with excitement. They know something, but they're afraid to tell me.

Mum gazed at me very seriously. "All right, Michael. We might as well tell you," she said. "We're all caught in a time warp, and there's nothing we can do about it."

Mum pushed back her chair. She walked backwards to the stove. She started dishing rice from her plate into the pot on the stove.

"Yenoh, ecir erom?" she asked Dad.

Huh?

"Esaelp, sey," Dad replied.

"Oot, em," Tara said. She spat some rice out on her fork and dumped it back on her plate. She was eating backwards!

Dad stood up and walked backwards to Mum. Then Tara skipped backwards around the kitchen table.

They were all talking and moving backwards. We really *were* in a time warp!

"Hey!" I cried. "It's true!"

Why wasn't I talking backwards, too?

"Norom," Tara said.

She cracked up first. Then Dad started laughing. Then Mum.

I finally caught on. It was a joke. "You—

you're all *horrible!*" I cried.

That made them laugh even more.

"I was wondering when you'd figure it out," Tara sneered.

They all sat down at the table again. Mum couldn't help grinning. "We're sorry, Michael. We didn't mean to make fun of you."

"Yes we did!" Tara exclaimed.

I stared at them in horror.

This was the most terrible thing that had ever happened to me. And my parents thought it was a big joke.

Then Dad said, "Michael, did you ever hear of *déjà vu?*"

I shook my head.

"It's when something happens to you and you have the feeling it's happened before," he explained. "Everyone feels that way once in a while. It's nothing to be afraid of."

"Maybe you're nervous about something," Mum added. "Like your birthday coming up. I'll bet you're a little nervous about turning twelve, right? And planning your party and everything?"

"Not really," I protested. "I know that feeling. But this isn't the same thing! This is—"

"Say, Mike," Dad interrupted. "Wait till you see what I got you for your birthday. You're going to flip! It's a big surprise."

No, it isn't, I thought unhappily.

It's not a surprise at all. You've given me that birthday present twice already. How many times are you going to give me that stupid bike?

"Mum, Michael is hiding peas in his napkin again," Tara ratted.

I smushed the peas up in my napkin and threw it in her face.

When I went to school the next morning, I wasn't sure what day it was. It was getting hard to keep track. My classes, my lunch, the stuff my friends said all seemed familiar. But nothing unusual happened. It could have been any day of the school year.

I played basketball after school that day, as usual. While I was playing, a funny feeling crept over me.

A bad feeling.

I've already played this game, I realized. And it didn't end well.

But I kept on playing, waiting to see what would happen.

My team won. We collected our packs.

Then Kevin Flowers yelled, "Where's my Blue Devils cap?"

Oh, yeah, I remembered.

This was *that* basketball game. How could I forget?

Good old Tara. She's done it again!

"Nobody leaves until we find that cap!"

I shut my eyes and handed over my pack.

I knew what was coming. Might as well get it over with.

Getting pounded to a pulp by Kevin Flowers hurt a lot. But at least the pain didn't last long.

The next morning when I woke up, it was all gone. The pain, the scabs, the bruises, everything.

What day is it today? I wondered. It must be a few days before Kevin beat me up.

I hope I won't have to live through that a third time.

But what will happen today?

As I walked to school, I searched for clues. I tried to remember what had happened a day or two before Kevin beat me up.

A maths test? Maybe. I hoped not. But at least it would be easier this time around. I could even try to remember what the problems were and look up all the answers before the test!

I was a little late today. Did that mean something? I wondered. Would I get into trouble?

My form teacher, Ms Jacobson, had closed the classroom door. I opened it. The classroom was already full.

Ms Jacobson didn't look up when I walked in.

I must not be that late, I thought. Guess I won't get in trouble after all.

I started for the back of the room, where I usually sit. As I passed through the rows of desks, I glanced at the other kids.

Who's that guy? I wondered, staring at a chubby, blond kid I'd never seen before.

Then I noticed a pretty girl with cornrows and three earrings in one ear. I'd never seen her before, either.

I stared at all the faces in the classroom. None of the kids looked familiar.

What's going on? I wondered, feeling panic choke my throat.

I don't know *any* of these kids!

Where's my class?

Ms Jacobson finally turned around. She stared at me.

"Hey," the blond kid shouted. "What's a third-grader doing in here?"

Everybody laughed. I couldn't understand why.

A third-grader? Who was he talking about?

I didn't see any third-graders.

"You're in the wrong classroom, young man," Ms Jacobson said to me. She opened the door, showing me the way out.

"I think your room is downstairs on the second floor," she added.

"Thanks," I said. I didn't know what she was talking about. But I decided to go along with her.

She shut the door behind her. I could hear the kids laughing behind the door. I hurried down the hall to the boy's bathroom. I needed to splash some cold water on my face. Maybe that would help.

I turned on the cold water tap. Then I glanced in the mirror, very quickly.

The mirror seems a little higher than usual, I thought.

I washed my hands in the cold water and splashed some on my face.

The sink seems higher, too, I noticed. Strange.

Am I in the right school?

I glanced in the mirror again—and got the shock of my life.

Was that *me*?

I looked so *young*.

I ran my head through my short, brushlike brown hair. That dopey crew cut I'd had all through the third grade.

I don't believe it, I thought, shaking my head. I'm a third-grader again!

I've got my third-grade hair. My third-grade clothes. My third-grade body.

But my seventh-grade brain. I think.

Third grade.

That means I've slipped back four years—in one night.

My whole body started to tremble. I grabbed on to the sink to steady myself.

I was suddenly paralysed with fear.

Things were speeding up. Now I'd lost whole years in one night! How old will I be when I wake up tomorrow? I asked myself.

Time was going backward faster and faster—

and I still hadn't found a way to stop it!

I shut off the water and dried my face with a paper towel. I didn't know what to do. I was so frightened, I couldn't think straight.

I walked back to my third-grade classroom.

First I glanced through the window of the classroom door. There she was, Mrs Harris, my old third-grade teacher. I'd know that helmet of silver hair anywhere.

And I knew, as soon as I saw her, that I really *had* gone back in time four years.

Because old Mrs Harris shouldn't have been in school that day. She'd retired two years earlier. When I was in fifth grade.

I opened the door and stepped into the classroom.

Mrs Harris didn't bat an eye. "Take a seat, Michael," she commanded. She never mentioned the fact that I was late.

Mrs Harris always liked me.

I checked out the other kids in the class. I saw Henry, Josh, Ceecee and Mona, all little third-graders now.

Mona wore her shiny brown hair in two braids. Ceecee wore hers in one of those stupid side ponytails.

Josh didn't have pimples on his forehead, I noticed. Henry had a sticker on the back of his hand—Donatello, from the Teenage Mutant Hero Turtles.

It was my class all right.

I sat down at an empty desk in the back. My old desk. Right next to Henry.

I glanced at him. He was picking his nose.

Gross. I'd forgotten about that part of being a third-grader.

"Michael, we're on page thirty-three in your spelling book," Mrs Harris informed me.

I reached inside the desk and found my spelling book. I opened it to page thirty-three.

"These are the words you'll need to know for tomorrow's spelling test," Mrs Harris announced. She wrote the words on the board, even though we could read them right there in the spelling book: *Taste, sense, grandmother, easy, happiness.*

"Man," Henry whispered to me. "These words are tough. Look how many letters there are in *grandmother!*"

I didn't know what to say to him. On my last spelling test (when I was still in the seventh grade), I'd had to spell *psychology. Grandmother* wasn't a big challenge for me any more.

I zoned out for most of the day. I'd always wished school were easier, but not *this* easy. It was so babyish and boring.

Lunch and break were even worse. Josh chewed up a banana and stuck his tongue out at me. Henry painted his face with chocolate pudding.

69

Finally the school day ended. I dragged my little third-grade body home.

When I opened the front door, I heard a horrible screech. Bubba, just a kitten now, raced past me and out the door. Tara toddled after him.

"Don't tease the cat," I scolded her.

"You're dumb," she replied.

I stared at Tara. She was three years old.

I tried to remember. Had I liked her better when she was three?

"Give me a piggyback!" she cried, tugging on my backpack.

"Get off me," I said.

My pack dropped to the floor. I stooped to pick it up. She grabbed a hunk of my hair and yanked it.

"Ow!" I screamed.

She laughed and laughed.

"That hurt!" I yelled, and shoved her—just as Mum stepped into the hall.

She rushed to Tara's side. "Michael, don't shove your sister. She's only a little girl!"

I stormed off to my room to think.

No, I *hadn't* liked Tara better when she was three. She was as much of a brat as ever.

She was born a brat, and she'd never grow out of it, I knew. She'd be a brat for the rest of her life, driving me crazy even when we're old.

If we ever get to be old, I thought with a

70

shudder. We'll *never* grow up at this rate.

What am I going to do? I worried. I've slipped back in time four years! If I don't do something fast, I'll be a baby again.

And then what?

A cold shiver ran down my back.

And then what? I asked myself.

Will I disappear *completely*?

I woke up in a panic every morning.

What day was it? What *year* was it?

I had no idea.

I climbed out of bed—it seemed farther away from the floor than it used to—and padded across the hall to the bathroom.

I stared in the mirror. How old was I? Younger than I'd been the day before, I knew that much.

I went back to my room and began to get dressed. Mum had left my clothes for the day folded on a chair in my room.

I examined the jeans I was supposed to wear. They had a picture of a cowboy on the back pocket.

Oh, yeah, I remembered. *These* jeans. The cowboy jeans.

Second grade.

That means I must be seven years old now.

I stepped into the trousers, thinking, I can't believe I have to wear these stupid jeans again.

Then I unfolded the shirt Mum had picked out for me.

My heart sank when I saw it: A cowboy shirt— with fringe and everything.

This is so embarrassing, I thought. How could I have ever let Mum do this to me?

Deep down I knew that I used to like these clothes. I probably picked them out myself.

But I couldn't stand to admit that I'd ever been so stupid.

Downstairs, Tara was still in her pyjamas, watching cartoons. She was now two.

When she saw me pass through the living room, she held out her arms to me. "Kiss! Kiss!" she called.

She wanted me to kiss her? That didn't seem like Tara.

But maybe the two-year-old Tara was still sweet and innocent. Maybe, at two, Tara was actually likeable.

"Kiss! Kiss!" she begged.

"Give poor Tara a kiss," Mum called from the kitchen. "You're her big brother, Michael. She looks up to you."

I sighed. "Okay."

I leaned down to give Tara a kiss on the cheek. With one chubby index finger, she poked me in the eye.

"Ow!" I shrieked.

Tara laughed.

73

Same old terrible Tara, I thought as I stumbled into the kitchen, one hand over my sore eye.

She was born bad!

This time, at school, I knew which classroom to go to.

There sat all my old friends, Mona and everybody, younger than ever. I'd forgotten how dopey everybody used to look when we were little.

I sat through another dull day of learning stuff I already knew. Subtraction. How to read books with really big print. Perfecting my capital L.

At least it gave me lots of time to think.

Every day I tried to figure out what to do. But I never came up with an answer.

Then I remembered Dad telling us he'd been wanting the cuckoo clock for fifteen years.

Fifteen years! That's it! The clock must be at that antique shop!

I'll go and find the clock, I decided. I couldn't wait for school to end that day.

I figured if I could turn the cuckoo around, time would go forward again. I knew the dial that showed the year must be going backwards, too. All I had to do was reset the date on the clock to the right year, and I'd be twelve again.

I missed being twelve. Seven-year-olds don't

get away with much. Someone's always watching you.

When the school day ended, I started down the block towards my house. I knew the crossing guard was watching me, making sure I'd get home safely.

But at the second block I dashed around the corner to the bus stop. I hoped the crossing guard hadn't seen me.

I stood behind a tree, trying not to be seen.

A few minutes later, a bus pulled over. The doors opened with a hiss. I stepped aboard.

The bus driver eyed me strangely. "Aren't you a little young to be catching the bus by yourself?" he asked me.

"Mind your own business," I replied.

He looked startled, so I added, "I'm meeting Daddy at his office. Mummy said it was okay."

He nodded and let the doors slide shut.

I started to put three quarters in the coin slot, but the driver stopped me after two.

"Whoa, there, buddy," he said, pressing the third quarter into my palm. "Fare's only fifty cents. Keep this quarter for a phone call."

"Oh, yeah. Right." I'd forgotten. They raised the bus fare to 75 cents when I was eleven. But now I was only seven. I put the quarter in my pocket.

The bus pulled away from the kerb and chugged downtown.

I remembered hearing Dad say that Anthony's Antiques and Stuff was across the street from his office. I got off the bus at Dad's block.

I hoped Dad wouldn't see me. I knew I'd be in big trouble if he did.

I wasn't allowed to catch the bus by myself when I was seven.

I hurried past Dad's building and crossed the street. On the corner stood a construction site; just a pile of bricks and rubble, really. Further down the block I saw a black sign with ANTHONY's ANTIQUES AND STUFF painted on it in gold letters.

My heart began to pound.

I'm almost there, I thought. Soon everything will be all right.

I'll just walk into the shop and find the clock. Then, when no one's looking, I'll turn the cuckoo around and fix the year.

I won't have to worry about waking up tomorrow morning as a three-year-old or something. My life will go back to normal.

Life will seem so easy, I told myself, when time is moving forward the way it's supposed to. Even *with* Tara around!

I gazed through the big plate glass window of the shop. There it stood, right in the window. The clock.

My palms began to sweat, I felt so excited.

I hurried to the shop door and turned the handle.

It wouldn't move. I jiggled it harder.

The door was locked.

Then I noticed a sign, tucked in the bottom corner of the door.

It said, CLOSED FOR VACATION.

I let out a howl of frustration. "NOOO!" I cried. Tears sprang to my eyes. "No! Not after all this."

I banged my head against the door. I couldn't stand it.

Closed for vacation.

How could I have such terrible luck?

How long was Anthony planning to be on vacation? I wondered. How long will the shop be closed?

By the time it reopens, I could be a baby!

I gritted my teeth and thought, there's no way I'm letting that happen. No way!

I've got to do something. *Anything.*

I pressed my nose against the shop window. The cuckoo clock was standing there, a metre or so in front of me.

And I couldn't get to it.

The window stood between me and that clock.

The window . . .

Normally, I would never think of doing what I decided to do at that moment.

But I was desperate. I had to reach that clock.

It really was a matter of life and death!

I strolled down the block to the construction site, trying to look casual. Trying not to look like a kid who was planning to break a shop window.

I stuffed my hands in the pockets of my cowboy jeans and whistled. I was sort of grateful to be wearing this stupid cowboy outfit after all. It made me look innocent.

Who would suspect a seven-year-old in a cowboy suit of trying to break into an antique shop?

I kicked around a little dirt at the construction site. Kicked a few rocks. Nobody seemed to be working there.

Slowly I made my way over to a pile of bricks. I glanced around to see if anybody saw me.

The coast was clear.

I picked up a brick and hefted it in my hand. It was very heavy. It wouldn't be easy for me, in my little second-grade body, to throw it far.

But I didn't have to throw it far. Just through the window.

I tried stuffing the brick in my jeans pocket, but it was too big. So I carried it in both hands back to the shop.

I tried to look as if it were perfectly normal for a boy to be carrying a brick down the street.

A few adults quickly passed by. No one gave me a second glance.

I stood in front of the shiny plate glass window, weighing the brick in my hand. I wondered if a burglar alarm would go off when I broke the window.

Would I be arrested?

Maybe it wouldn't matter. If I made time to go to the present, I'd escape the police.

Be brave, I told myself. Go for it!

With both hands, I raised the brick over my head . . .

. . . and someone grabbed me from behind.

"Help!" I shouted. I spun around. "Dad!"

"Michael, what are you doing here?" Dad demanded. "Are you by yourself?"

I let the brick fall to the pavement. He didn't seem to see it.

"I—I wanted to surprise you," I lied. "I wanted to come and visit you after school."

He stared at me as if he didn't quite understand. So I added, for good measure, "I missed you, Daddy."

He smiled. "You missed me?" He was touched. I could tell.

"How did you get here?" he asked. "On the bus?"

I nodded.

"You know you're not allowed to go on the bus by yourself," he said. But he didn't sound angry. I knew that line about missing him would soften him up.

Meanwhile, I still had the same major

problem—getting my hands on the cuckoo clock.

Could Dad help me? Would he? I was willing to try anything. "Dad," I said, "that clock—"

Dad put his arm around me. "Isn't it a beauty? I've been admiring it for years."

"Dad, I've got to get to the clock," I insisted. "It's very, very important! Do you know when the store will open again? We've got to get that clock somehow!"

Dad misunderstood me. He patted me on the head and said, "I know how you feel, Michael. I wish I could have the clock right now. But I can't afford it. Maybe some day . . ."

He pulled me away from the shop. "Come on— let's go home. I wonder what's for supper tonight?"

I didn't say another word all the way home in the car. All I could think about was the clock— and what would happen to me next.

How old will I be when I wake up tomorrow? I wondered.

Or how young?

When I opened my eyes the next morning, everything had changed.

The walls were painted baby blue. The bedspread and the curtains matched. The material was printed with bouncing kangaroos. On one wall hung a needlepoint picture of a cow.

It wasn't my room, but it looked familiar.

Then I felt a lump in the bed. I reached under the kangaroo covers and pulled out Harold, my old teddy bear.

I slowly understood. I was back in my old bedroom.

How had I ended up there? It was Tara's room now.

I jumped out of bed. I was wearing smurf pyjamas.

I swear I don't remember ever liking smurfs that much.

I ran to the bathroom to look in the mirror.

How old was I now?

I couldn't tell. I had to stand on the toilet seat to see my face.

A bad sign.

Yikes. I looked about five years old!

I hopped off the toilet seat and hurried downstairs.

"Hello, Mikey," Mum said, squeezing me and giving me a big kiss.

"Hi, Mummy," I said. I couldn't believe how babyish my voice sounded.

Dad sat at the kitchen table, drinking coffee. He put down his mug and held out his arms. "Come give Daddy a good morning kiss," he said.

I sighed and forced myself to run into his arms and kiss him on the cheek. I'd forgotten how many stupid things little kids have to put up with.

I ran out of the kitchen on my little five-year-old legs, through the living room, into the den, and back to the kitchen. Something was missing.

No, some*one* was missing.

Tara.

"Sit still for a minute, sweetie," Mum said, scooping me up and plopping me into a chair. "Want some cereal?"

"Where's Tara?" I demanded.

"Who?" Mum replied.

"Tara," I repeated.

84

Mum glanced at Dad. Dad shrugged.

"You know," I persisted. "My little sister."

Mum smiled. "Oh, *Tara*," she said, seeming to understand at last.

She glanced at Dad and mouthed, "Invisible friend."

"Huh?" Dad said out loud. "He has an invisible friend?"

Mum frowned at him and gave me a bowl of cereal. "What does your friend Tara look like, Mikey?"

I didn't answer her. I was too shocked to speak.

They don't know who I'm talking about! I realized.

Tara don't exist. She hasn't been born yet!

For a brief moment, I felt a thrill. No Tara! I could go through this whole day without ever seeing, hearing, or smelling Tara the Terrible! How totally awesome!

But then the real meaning of this sank in.

One Webster kid had disappeared.

I was next.

After I'd finished my cereal, Mum took me upstairs to get dressed. She put on my shirt and trousers and socks and shoes. She didn't tie the shoes, though.

"Okay, Mikey," she said. "Let's practise tying your shoes. Remember how we did it yesterday?"

She took my shoelaces in her fingers and, as she tied them, chanted. "The bunny hops *around* the tree and ducks *under* the bush. Remember?"

She sat back to watch me try to tie my other shoe. I could tell by the look on her face she didn't expect me to get very far.

I bent over and easily tied the shoe. I didn't have time to fool around with this stuff.

Mum stared at me in amazement.

"Come on, Mum, let's get going," I said, straightening up.

"Mikey!" Mum cried. "You did it! You tied your shoe for the first time!" She grabbed me and hugged me hard. "Wait till I tell Daddy!"

I followed her downstairs, rolling my eyes.

So I tied my shoe. Big deal!

"Honey!" Mum called. "Mikey tied his shoe—all by himself!"

"Hey!" Dad cried happily. He held up one hand so I could slap him five. "That's my big boy!"

This time I saw him mouth to Mum: "Took him long enough!"

I was too worried to be insulted.

Mum walked me to nursery school. She told my teacher that I'd learned to tie my shoe. Big excitement all around.

I had to sit around that stupid nursery all morning, finger-painting and singing the ABC song.

I knew I had to get back to that antique store. It was all I could think about.

I've *got* to change that cuckoo clock, I thought desperately. Who knows? Tomorrow I might not know how to walk.

But how would I get there? It had been hard enough to get into town as a second-grader. As a five-year-old, it would be nearly impossible.

And, besides, even if I could get on the bus without anybody asking questions, I didn't have any money with me.

I glanced at the teacher's purse. Maybe I could steal a couple of quarters from her. She'd probably never know.

But if she caught me, I'd be in really big trouble. And I had enough trouble now.

I decided to sneak on to the bus somehow. I knew I could find a way.

When the nursery torture was finally over for the day, I raced out of the building to catch the bus—

—and bumped smack into Mum.

"Hi, Mikey," she said. "Did you have a nice day?"

I forgot that she picked me up every day from nursery school.

She took my hand in her iron grip. There was no escape.

At least I'm here, I thought when I woke up the next morning. At least I'm still alive.

But I'm four years old.

Time is running out.

Mum waltzed into my room, singing, "Good morning to you, good morning to you, good morning dear Mikey, good morning to you! Ready for playgroup?"

Yuck. Playgroup.

Things kept getting worse and worse.

I couldn't take it any more. Mum dropped me off at playgroup with a kiss and her usual, "Have a nice day, Mikey!"

I stalked to the nearest corner and sat. I watched the other little kids play. I refused to do anything. No singing. No painting. No sandbox. No games for me.

"Michael, what's the matter with you today?" the teacher, Ms Sarton asked. "Don't you feel well?"

"I feel okay," I told her.

"Well, then, why aren't you playing?" She studied me for a minute, then added, "I think you need to play."

Without asking my permission or anything, she picked me up, carried me outside, and dumped me in the sandbox.

"Mona will play with you," she said brightly.

Mona was very cute when she was four. Why didn't I remember that?

Mona didn't say anything to me. She concentrated on the sand igloo she was building—at least I *think* it was supposed to be an igloo. It was round, anyway. I started to say hi to her, but suddenly felt shy.

Then I caught myself. Why should I feel bashful with a four-year-old girl?

Anyway, I reasoned, she hasn't seen me in my underwear yet. That won't happen for another eight years.

"Hi, Mona," I said. I cringed when I heard the babyish playgroup voice that came out of my mouth. But everyone else seemed to be used to it.

Mona turned up her nose. "Eeew," she sniffed. "A boy. I hate boys."

"Well," I squeaked in my little boy voice, "if that's the way you feel, forget I said anything."

Mona stared at me now, as if she didn't quite understand what I had said.

"You're stupid," she said.

I shrugged and began to draw swirls in the sand with my chubby little finger. Mona dug a moat around her sand igloo. Then she stood up. "Don't let anybody smash my sand castle," she ordered.

So it wasn't an igloo. Guess I was wrong.

"Okay," I agreed.

She toddled away. A few minutes later she returned, carrying a bucket.

She carefully poured a little water into her sand castle moat. She dumped the rest on my head.

"Stupid boy!" she squealed, running away.

I rose and shook my wet head like a dog. I felt a strange urge to burst into tears and run to the teacher for help, but I fought it.

Mona stood a few metres away from me, ready to run. "*Nyah nyah!*" she taunted. "Come and get me, Mikey!"

I pushed my wet hair out of my face and stared at Mona.

"You can't catch me!" she called.

What could I do? I had to chase after her.

I began to run. Mona screamed and raced to a tree by the playground fence. Another girl stood there. Was that Ceecee?

She wore thick glasses with pink rims, and underneath, a pink eyepatch.

I'd forgotten about that eyepatch. She'd had to wear it until halfway through first grade.

Mona screamed again and clutched at Ceecee. Ceecee clutched her back and screamed, too.

I stopped in front of the tree. "Don't worry. I won't hurt you," I assured them.

"Yes you will!" Mona squealed. "Help!"

I sat down on the grass to prove I didn't want to hurt them.

"He's hurting us! He's hurting us!" the girls shouted. They unclutched their hands and jumped on top of me.

"Ow!" I cried.

"Hold his arms!" Mona ordered. Ceecee obeyed. Mona started tickling me under the arms.

"Stop it!" I begged. It was torture. "Stop it!"

"No!" Mona cried. "That's what you get for trying to catch us!"

"I . . . didn't . . ." I had trouble getting the words out while she tickled me. "I didn't . . . try to . . ."

"Yes you did!" Mona insisted.

I'd forgotten that Mona used to be so bossy. It made me think twice. If I ever make it back to my real age, I thought, maybe I won't like Mona so much any more.

"Please stop," I begged again.

"I'll stop," Mona said. "But only if you promise something."

"What?"

"You have to climb that tree." She pointed to the tree by the fence. "Okay?"

I stared at the tree. Climbing it wouldn't be such a big deal. "Okay," I agreed. "Just get off me!"

Mona stood up. Ceecee let go of my arms.

I climbed to my feet and brushed the grass off my trousers.

"You're scared," Mona taunted.

"I am not!" I replied. What a brat! She was almost as bad as Tara!

Now Mona and Ceecee chanted, "Mikey is scared. Mikey is scared."

I ignored them. I grabbed the lowest branch of the tree and hauled myself up. It was harder than I thought it would be. My four-year-old body wasn't very athletic.

"Mikey is scared. Mikey is scared."

"Shut up!" I yelled down at them. "Can't you see that I'm climbing the stupid tree? It doesn't make sense to tease me about being scared."

They both gave me that blank look Mona had given me before. As if they didn't understand what I was saying.

"Mikey is scared," they chanted again.

I sighed and kept climbing. My hands were so small, it was hard to grip the branches. One of my feet slipped.

Then a terrible thought popped into my head.

Wait a minute.

I shouldn't be doing this.

Isn't playgroup the year I broke my arm?

YEEEEOOOOOOWWWWW!

Morning again.

I yawned and opened my eyes. I shook my left arm, the one I broke climbing that stupid tree the day before.

The arm felt fine. Perfectly normal. Completely healed.

I must have gone back in time again, I thought. That's the good part about this messed-up time thing: I didn't have to wait for my arm to heal.

I wondered how far back I'd gone.

The sun poured in through the window of Tara's—or my—room. It cast a weird shadow across my face: a striped shadow.

I tried to roll out of bed. My body slammed against something.

What was that? I rolled back to look.

Bars!

I was surrounded by bars! Was I in jail?

I tried to sit up so I could see better. It wasn't as

easy as usual. My stomach muscles seemed to have grown weak.

At last I managed to sit up and look around.

I wasn't in jail. I was in a cot!

Crumpled up beside me was my old yellow blankie with the embroidered duck on it. I sat beside a small pile of stuffed animals. I was wearing a tiny white undershirt, and—

Oh, no.

I shut my eyes in horror.

It can't be. Please don't let it be true! I prayed.

I opened my eyes and checked to see if my prayer had come true.

It hadn't.

I was wearing a nappy.

A nappy!

How young am I now? How far back in time did I go? I wondered.

"Are you awake, Mikey?"

Mum came into the room. She looked pretty young. I didn't remember ever seeing her this young before.

"Did you get lots of sleep, sweetie pie?" Mum asked. She clearly expected no answer from me. Instead, she shoved a bottle of juice into my mouth.

Yuck! A bottle!

I pulled it out of my mouth and clumsily threw it down.

Mum picked it up. "No, no," she said patiently.

95

"Bad little Mikey. Drink your bottle now. Come on."

She slid it back into my mouth. I *was* thirsty, so I drank the juice. Drinking from a bottle wasn't that bad, once you got used to it.

Mum left the room. I let the bottle drop.

I had to know how old I was. I had to find out how much time I had left.

I grabbed the bars of the cot and pulled myself to my feet.

Okay, I thought. I can stand.

I took a step. I couldn't control my leg muscles very well. I toddled around the cot.

I can walk, I realized. Unsteadily, but at least I can walk.

I must be about one year old!

I fell just then and banged my head against the side of the cot. Tears welled in my eyes. I started wailing, howling.

Mum ran into the room. "What's the matter, Mikey? What happened?"

She picked me up and started patting me on the back.

I couldn't stop crying. It was really embarrassing.

What am I going to do? I thought desperately. In one night, I went back in time three years!

I'm only one year old now. How old will I be tomorrow?

A little shiver ran down my tiny spine.

I've got to find a way to make time go forward again—today! I told myself.

But what can I do?

I'm not even in playgroup any more.

I'm a baby!

Mum said we were going out. She wanted to dress me. Then she uttered the dreaded words.

"I bet I know what's bothering you, Mikey. You probably need your nappy changed."

"No!" I cried. "No!"

"Oh, yes you do, Mikey. Come on . . ."

I don't like to think about what happened after that. I'd rather block it out of my memory.

I'm sure you understand.

When the worst was over, Mum plopped me down in a playpen—more bars—while she bustled around the house.

I shook a rattle. I batted at a model plane hanging over my head. I watched it spin around.

I pressed buttons on a plastic toy. Different noises came out when I pressed different buttons. A squeak. A honk. A moo.

I was bored out of my mind.

Then Mum picked me up again. She bundled

me into a warm sweater and a dopey little knit cap. Baby blue.

"Want to see Daddy?" she cooed at me. "Want to see Daddy and go shopping?"

"Da-da," I replied.

I'd planned to say, "If you don't take me to Anthony's Antiques, I'll throw myself out of my cot and crack my head open."

But I couldn't talk. It was so frustrating!

Mum carried me out to the car. She strapped me into a baby seat in the back. I tried to say, "Not so tight, Mum!" It came out, "No no no no no!"

"Don't give me a hard time now, Mikey," Mum said sharply. "I know you don't like your car seat, but it's the law." She gave the strap an extra tug.

Then she drove into town.

At least there's a chance, I thought. If we're going to meet Dad, we'll be near the antique store. Maybe, just maybe.

Mum parked the car outside Dad's office building. She unstrapped me from the car seat.

I could move again. But not for long. She pulled a pushchair out of the trunk, unfolded it, and strapped me in.

Being a baby really is like being a prisoner, I thought as she wheeled me across the pavement. I never realized how awful it is!

It was lunchtime. A stream of workers flowed out of the office building. Dad appeared and gave Mum a kiss.

He squatted down to tickle me under the chin. "There's my little boy!" he said.

"Can you say hi to your daddy?" Mum prompted me.

"Hi, Da-da," I gurgled.

"Hi, Mikey," Dad said fondly. But when we stood up, he spoke quietly to Mum, as if I couldn't hear. "Shouldn't he being saying more words by now, honey? Ted Jackson's kid is Mikey's age, and he can say whole sentences. He can say 'lightbulb' and 'kitchen' and 'I want my teddy bear.'"

"Don't start that again," Mum whispered angrily. "Mikey is *not* slow."

I squirmed in my pushchair, fuming. Slow! Who said I was slow?

"I didn't say he was slow, honey," Dad went on. "I only said—"

"Yes you did," Mum insisted. "Yes you did! The other night, when he stuffed those peas up his nose, you said you thought we should have him tested!"

I stuffed peas up my nose? I shuddered.

Sure, stuffing peas up your nose is stupid. But I was only a baby. Wasn't Dad getting carried away?

I thought so.

I wished I could tell them I would turn out all right—at least up to the age of twelve. I mean, I'm no genius, but I get mostly A's and B's.

"Can we discuss this later?" Dad said. "I've only got an hour for lunch. If we're going to find a dining room table, we'd better get moving."

"*You* brought it up," Mum sniffed. She wheeled the pushchair smartly around and began to cross the street. Dad followed us.

I let my eyes rove along the shop windows across the street. An apartment building. A pawnshop. A coffee shop.

Then I found what I was looking for: Anthony's Antiques and Stuff.

My heart leaped. The store still existed! I kept my eyes glued to that sign.

Please take me in there, Mum, I silently prayed. Please please please!

Mum steered me down the street. Past the apartment building. Past the pawnshop. Past the coffee shop.

We stopped in front of Anthony's. Dad stood in front of the window, hands in his pockets, gazing through the glass. Mum and I pulled up beside him.

I couldn't believe it. Finally, after all this time—some good luck!

I stared through the window, searching for it.

101

The clock.

The window display was set up like an old-fashioned living room. My eyes roamed over the furniture: a wooden bookcase, a fringed table lamp, a Persian rug, an overstuffed armchair, and a clock . . . a table clock. Not the cuckoo clock.

Not the right clock.

My heart sank back to its normal low spot in my chest.

It figures, I thought. Here I am, at the antique shop, at last.

And the clock isn't here.

I felt like crying.

I could have cried, too. Easily.

After all, I was a baby. People expected me to cry.

But I didn't. Even though I looked like a baby, I was a twelve-year-old inside. I still had my pride.

Dad stepped to the door and held it open for Mum and me. Mum pushed me inside. I sat strapped into the pushchair.

The shop was jammed with old furniture. A chubby man in his forties strolled down the aisle towards us.

Behind him, down at the end of the aisle, in a corner at the back of the shop, I saw it. The clock. *The* clock.

A squeal of excitement popped out of me. I began to rock in my pram. I was so close!

"May I help you?" the man asked Mum and Dad.

"We're looking for a dining room table," Mum told him.

I had to get out of that pushchair. I had to get to that clock.

I rocked harder, but it was no good. I was strapped in. "Let me out of this thing!" I shouted.

Mum and Dad turned to look at me. "What's he saying?" Dad asked.

"It sounded like 'La ma la ma'," the shopkeeper suggested.

I rocked harder than ever and screamed.

"He hates his pushchair," Mum explained. She leaned down and unbuckled the straps. "I'll hold him for a few minutes. Then he'll quieten down."

I waited until she held me in her arms. Then I screamed again and wriggled as hard as I could.

Dad's face reddened. "Michael, what is wrong with you?"

"Down! Down!" I yelled.

"All right," Mum muttered, setting me down on the floor. "Now please stop screaming."

I quietened down immediately. I tested my wobbly, chubby little legs. They wouldn't get me far, but they were all I had to work with.

"Keep an eye on him," the shopkeeper warned. "A lot of this stuff is breakable."

Mum grabbed my hand. "Come on, Mikey. Let's go look at some tables."

She tried to lead me to a corner of the shop where several wooden tables stood. I whined and squirmed, hoping to get away. Her grip was too tight.

"Mikey, *shh*," she said.

I let her drag me to the tables. I glanced up at the cuckoo clock. It was almost noon.

At noon, I knew, the cuckoo would pop out. It was my only chance to grab the bird and turn it around.

I tugged on Mum's hand. She tightened her grip.

"What do you think of this one, honey?" Dad asked her, rubbing his hand along a dark wood table.

"I think that wood's too dark for our chairs, Herman," Mum said. Another table caught her eye. As she moved towards it, I tried to slip my hand out of hers. No go.

I toddled after her to the second table. I shot another glance at the clock. The minute hand moved.

Two minutes to twelve.

"We can't be too picky, honey," Dad said. "The Bergers are coming over Saturday night—two days from now—for a dinner party. We can't have a dinner party without a dining room table!"

"I *know* that, dear. But there's no point in buying a table we don't like."

Dad's voice began to rise. Mum's mouth got that hard, set look to it.

Aha. A fight. This was my chance.

Dad was shouting. "Why don't we just spread a blanket out on the floor and make them eat there? We'll call it a picnic!"

Mum finally relaxed her grip on my hand.

I slipped away and toddled as fast as I could towards the clock.

The clock's minute hand moved again.

I toddled faster.

I heard my parents shouting at each other. "I won't buy an ugly table, and that's that!" Mum cried.

Please don't let them notice me, I prayed. Not yet.

I reached the cuckoo clock at last. I stood in front of it and stared up at the clock.

The cuckoo's window was far above me, out of reach.

The minute hand clicked again. The clock's gong sounded.

The cuckoo's window slid open. The cuckoo popped out.

It cuckooed once.

It cuckooed twice.

I stared up at it, helpless.

A twelve-year-old boy trapped in a baby's body.

I stared grimly up at the clock.

Somehow, I had to reach that cuckoo.

Somehow, I *had* to turn it around.

Cuckoo! Cuckoo!

Three, four.

I knew that once it reached twelve, I was doomed.

The cuckoo bird would disappear.

And so would my last chance to save myself.

In a day or so, I would disappear. Disappear for ever.

Frantic, I glanced around for a ladder, a stool, anything.

The closest thing was a chair.

I toddled over to the chair and pushed it towards the clock. It moved a few centimetres.

I leaned, putting all my weight into it. I figured I weighed about twenty pounds.

But it was enough. The chair began to slide across the floor.

Cuckoo! Cuckoo! Five, six.

I shoved the chair up against the clock. The seat of the chair came up to my chin.

I tried to pull myself up on to the seat. My arms were too weak.

I planted a baby shoe against the chair leg. I boosted myself up. I grabbed a spindle at the back of the chair and heaved my body on to the seat.

I made it!

Cuckoo! Cuckoo! Seven, eight.

I got to my knees. I got to my feet.

I reached up to grab the cuckoo. I stretched as tall as I could.

Cuckoo! Cuckoo! Nine, ten.

Reaching, reaching.

Then I heard the shopkeeper shout, "Somebody grab that baby!"

I heard pounding footsteps.

They were running to get me.

I strained to reach the cuckoo. Just another inch . . .

Cuckoo!

Eleven.

Mum grabbed me. She lifted me up.

For one second, the cuckoo flashed within my reach.

I grasped it and turned the head around.

Cuckoo!

Twelve.

The cuckoo slid back into the clock, facing the right way.

Forward.

I wriggled out of Mum's arms, landing on the chair.

"Mikey, what's got into you?" she cried. She tried to grab me again.

I dodged her. I reached around to the side of the clock.

I saw the little dial that told the year. I felt for the button that controlled it. I could just reach it, standing on the chair.

I slammed my hand on the button, carefully watching the years whiz by.

I heard the shopkeeper yelling, "Get that baby away from my clock!"

Mum grabbed me again, but I screamed. I screamed so loudly, it startled her. She let her hands drop.

"Mikey, let go of that!" Dad ordered.

I took my hand off the button. The dial showed the right year. The present year. The year I turned twelve.

Mum made another grab for me. This time I let her pick me up.

It doesn't matter what happens now, I thought. Either the clock will work, and I'll go back to being twelve again . . .

. . . or else it won't work. And then what?

Then I'll disappear. Vanish in time. For ever.

I waited.

"I'm so sorry," Dad said to the shopkeeper. "I hope the baby didn't damage the clock."

The muscles in my neck tensed.

Nothing was happening. Nothing.

I waited another minute.

The shopkeeper inspected the clock. "Everything seems okay," he told Dad. "But he's changed the year. I'll have to change it back."

"NO!" I wailed. "No! Don't!"

"That boy could use a little discipline, if you ask me," the shopkeeper said.

He reached his hand around the side of the clock and started to set back the year.

"Nooo!" I wailed. "Nooo!"

That's it, I realized. I'm doomed. I'm a goner.

But the shopkeeper never touched the button.

A bright white light flashed. I felt dizzy, stunned. I blinked. And blinked again.

Several seconds passed before I could see anything.

I felt cool, damp air. I smelled at a musty odour. A garage smell.

"Michael? Do you like it?" Dad's voice.

I blinked. My eyes adjusted. I saw Dad and Mum. Looking older. Looking *normal*.

We were standing in the garage. Dad was holding a shiny new 21-speed bike.

Mum frowned. "Michael, are you feeling all right?"

They were giving me the bike. It was my birthday!

The clock worked! I'd brought myself back to the present!

Almost to the present. Up to my twelfth birthday.

Close enough.

I felt so happy, I thought I'd explode.

I threw myself at Mum and hugged her hard. Then I hugged Dad.

"Wow," Dad gushed. "I guess you really *do* like the bike!"

I grinned. "I love it!" I exclaimed. "I love everything! I love the whole world!"

Mainly, I loved being twelve again. I could walk! I could talk! I could ride the bus by myself!

Whoa! Wait a minute, I thought. It's my birthday.

Don't tell me I have to live through it *again*.

I tensed my shoulders and steeled myself for the horrible day to come.

It's worth it, I told myself. It's worth it if it means time will go forward again, the way it's supposed to.

I knew too well what would happen next.

Tara.

She'd try to get on my bike. The bike would fall over and get scratched.

Okay, Tara, I thought. I'm ready. Come and do your worst.

I waited.

Tara didn't come.

In fact, she didn't seem to be around at all.

114

She wasn't in the garage. No sign of her.

Mum and Dad *oohed* and *ahhed* over the bike. They didn't act as if anything was wrong. Or anyone was missing.

"Where's Tara?" I asked them.

They looked up.

"Who?" They stared at me.

"Did you invite her to your party?" Mum asked. "I don't remember sending an invitation to a Tara."

Dad grinned at me. "Tara? Is that some girl you have a crush on, Michael?"

"No," I answered, turning red.

It was as if they'd never heard of Tara. Never heard of their own daughter.

"You'd better go upstairs and get ready for your party, Michael," Mum suggested. "The kids will be here soon."

"Okay." I stumbled into the house, dazed.

"Tara?" I called.

Silence.

Could she be hiding somewhere?

I searched through the house. Then I checked her room. I threw open the door. I expected to see a messy, all-pink girl's room with a white canopy bed.

Instead, I saw two twin beds, neatly made with plaid covers. A chair. An empty closet. No personal stuff.

Not Tara's room.

A guest room.

Wow. I was amazed.

No Tara. Tara doesn't exist.

How did that happen?

I wandered into the den, looking for the cuckoo clock.

It wasn't there.

For a second, I felt a shock of fear. Then I calmed down.

Oh, yeah, I remembered. We don't have the clock yet. Not on my birthday. Dad bought it a couple of days later.

But I still didn't understand. What had happened to my little sister? Where was Tara?

My friends arrived for the party. We played CDs and ate tortilla chips. Ceecee pulled me into a corner and whispered that Mona had a crush on me.

Wow. I glanced at Mona. She turned a little pink and glanced away, shyly.

Tara wasn't there to embarrass me. It made a big difference.

My friends had all brought presents. I actually opened them myself. No Tara to open my presents before I got to them.

At cake time, I carried the cake into the dining room and set it in the middle of the table. No problem. I didn't fall and make a fool out of myself.

Because Tara wasn't there to trip me.

It was the greatest birthday party I'd ever had. It was probably the greatest *day* I'd ever lived— because Tara wasn't there to ruin it.

I could get used to this, I thought.

A few days later, the cuckoo clock was delivered to our house.

"Isn't it great?" Dad gushed, as he had the first time. "Anthony sold me the clock cheap. He said he'd discovered a tiny flaw on it."

The flaw. I'd almost forgotten about it.

We still didn't know what it was. But I couldn't help wondering if it had something to do with Tara's disappearance.

Maybe the clock didn't work perfectly in some way? Maybe it had somehow left Tara behind?

I hardly dared to touch the clock. I didn't want to set off any more weird time trips.

But I had to know what had happened.

I carefully studied the face of the clock again, and all the decorations. Then I stared at the dial that showed the year.

It was properly set at the current year.

Without really thinking about it, I scanned twelve places down the dial to find the year I was born.

There it was.

Then I scanned my eyes back up the dial. 1984. 1985. 1986. 1987. 1989 . . .

Wait a second.

Didn't I just skip a year?

I checked the dates again.

Nineteen-eighty-eight was missing. There was no 1988 on the dial.

And 1988 was the year Tara was born!

"Dad!" I cried. "I found the flaw! Look—there's a year missing on the dial."

Dad patted me on the back. "Good job, son! Wow, isn't that funny?"

To him it was just a funny mistake.

He had no idea his daughter had never been born.

I suppose there's some way to go back in time and get her.

I guess I probably ought to do that.

And I will.

Really.

One of these days.

Maybe.

Add *more*

Goosebumps

to your collection . . .
A chilling preview of
what's next from
R.L. Stine

Monster Blood III

"Don't do it!" Kermit shrieked in his scratchy mouse voice.

Conan raised a huge fist. With his other hand, he grabbed the front of Evan's T-shirt. He glared down at Kermit. "Why not?" he growled.

"Because I have *this*!" Kermit declared.

"Huh?" Conan let go of Evan's shirt. He stared at the glass beaker Kermit had raised in both hands. The beaker was half-full with a dark blue liquid.

Conan let out a sigh and swept a beefy hand back through his wavy blond hair. His blue eyes narrowed at Kermit. "What's that? Your baby formula?"

"Ha-ha," Kermit replied sarcastically.

If Kermit doesn't shut up, we're *both* going to get pounded! Evan realized. What is the little creep trying to do?

He tugged at Kermit's sleeve, trying to pull him away from Conan. But Kermit ignored him. He raised the beaker close to Conan's face.

"It's an Invisibility Mixture," Kermit said. "If I pour it on you, you'll disappear."

We should *both* disappear! Evan thought frantically. He let his eyes dart around the garden. Maybe I can make it through that hedge before Conan grabs me, he thought. If I can get around the next house and down to the street, I might escape.

But would it be right to leave little Kermit at Conan's mercy?

Evan sighed. He couldn't abandon his cousin like that. Evan though Kermit was definitely asking for it.

"You're going to make me invisible with that stuff?" Conan asked Kermit with a sneer.

Kermit nodded. "If I pour a few drops on you, you'll disappear. Really. I mixed it myself. It works. It's a mixture of Teflon dioxinate and magnesium parasulfidine."

"Yeah. Right," Conan muttered. He peered at the liquid in the beaker. "What makes it blue?"

"Food colouring," Kermit replied. Then he lowered his squeaky voice, trying to sound tough. "You'd better go home now, Conan. I don't want to have to use this stuff."

Oh, wow! Evan thought, pulling the bill of his Braves caps down over his face. I can't bear to watch this. This is sad. Really sad. Kermit is such a jerk.

"Go ahead. Try it," Evan heard Conan say.

Evan raised the cap so he could see. "Uh . . . Kermit . . . maybe we should go in the house now," he whispered.

"Go ahead. Make me invisible," Conan challenged.

"You really want me to?" Kermit demanded.

"Yeah," Conan replied. "I want to be invisible. I dare you."

Kermit raised the beaker over the grey muscle shirt that covered Conan's broad chest.

"Kermit—no!" Evan pleaded. "Don't! Please *don't!*"

Evan made a frantic grab for the beaker.

Too late.

Kermit turned the beaker over and let the thick blue liquid pour on to the front of Conan's shirt.